PHILADELPHIA EAGLES

A Story of Football Greatness

Melinda C. Bills

Copyright @ 2023 by Melinda C. Bills.

All rights reserved. No part of this book may be reproduced, distributed, or transmitted in any form or by any means, including photocopying, recording, or other electronic or mechanical methods, without the prior written permission of the publisher, except in the case of brief quotations embodied in critical reviews and certain other noncommercial uses permitted by copyright law.

This book is a work of fiction. Names, characters, places, and incidents either are products of the author's imagination or are used fictitiously. Any resemblance to actual events or locales or persons, living or dead, is entirely coincidental.

Table of Content

Introduction

Chapter 1: Team Origins and History
Early Years and Formation
Rise to Prominence: 1940s-1970s
Modern Era: 1980s to Present

Chapter 2: Key Players and Legends
Hall of Fame Players
Memorable Quarterbacks
Iconic Defensive Players

Chapter 3: Memorable Seasons and Championships
Super Bowl Triumphs
NFC Championships
Divisional Dominance

Chapter 4: The Eagles' Fanbase and Culture
Dedicated Fan Groups
Tailgating Traditions
Impact on Philadelphia's Community

Chapter 5: Iconic Rivalries
Historic Battles with Dallas Cowboys
Intense Matchups with the New York Giants
Fierce Feuds with Washington Football Team

Chapter 6: Behind the Scenes: Team Management
Coaching Dynasties
Front Office Strategies
Player Development and Drafting

Chapter 7: Impact on the NFL and Pop Culture
Eagles in Popular Media
Influence on NFL Policies
Eagles' Players in the Hall of Fame

Chapter 8: Looking Forward: Challenges and Aspirations
Recent Developments and Team Changes
Fan Expectations and Team Goals

Conclusion

Introduction

The Philadelphia Hawks, a robust establishment in the National Football League (NFL), stands as a demonstration of the energy, versatility, and immovable commitment that portray the soul of Philadelphia itself. Laid out in 1933, this celebrated group has cut a permanent blemish on the archives of American football, catching the hearts of millions with their determination, coarseness, and obvious ability. The Birds are not just a sports group; they are an image of solidarity, pride, and immovable assurance for their given fanbase, broadly known as the "Eagles Nation."

The group's journey to significance is cleared with a rich embroidery of wins and difficulties. Throughout the long term, the Falcons have endured the hardships of accidents, arising more grounded and more resolved each time. Their extraordinary minutes on the field have become scratched in the aggregate memory of football aficionados, with famous plays and amazing players characterizing their heritage. From the exhilarating triumphs to the deplorable losses, the Eagles have reliably exhibited their determination, exemplifying the embodiment of the city they address.

Philadelphia, a city eminent for its regular hard-working attitude and enthusiastic games culture, tracks down an impression of its character in The Eagles. The group's home arena, Lincoln Financial Field, resonates with the stunning cheers of fans wearing noon green, creating an electronic environment that powers the players' adrenaline and motivates wonder in observers. The kinship among fans, regularly alluded to as the "Eagles Family," rises above geological limits, joining individuals from different foundations under the flag of their common love for the game and the group.

Also, the Eagles' obligation to local area commitment and generosity has charmed them to the hearts of Philadelphians considerably further. Through different magnanimous drives and effort programs, the group has had a constructive outcome, supporting their job as competitors, but also, as powerful figures who contribute seriously to society.

As they keep on pre-arranging their legacy on the NFL stage, their process addresses something other than triumphs and losses. It represents the resolute soul of strength, the force of solidarity, and the victory of the human will. With each score scored and each challenge survived, the Philadelphia Eagles stand as an encouraging sign and motivation, helping every one of us to remember the phenomenal levels that can be accomplished through energy, devotion, and unshakeable conviction.

Chapter 1: Team Origins and History

In the records of any effective association, the journey of its arrangement and the set of experiences behind it are many times entrancing stories that shed light on the inspirations, difficulties, and achievements that have molded its advancement. The starting points and history of a group give a significant setting for understanding the elements and culture that characterize it.

Early Years and Formation

The Philadelphia Falcons, one of the NFL's most seasoned and most celebrated organizations, has a rich history tracing back to their foundation in 1933. Their initial years and development assumed a crucial part in forming the group's personality and heritage.

The Eagles were established by Bert Bell and Lud Wray, who, in a period of financial vulnerability during the Economic crisis of the early 20s, saw a chance to present another expert football crew to the city of Philadelphia. In a gathering held in 1933, the team's name was chosen, and the Philadelphia Eagles were conceived, motivated by the image of the American bald eagle, addressing strength, fortitude, and opportunity.

In their underlying years, the Eagles battled to make progress on the field. They played their home games at the Baker Bowl and later at the Philadelphia Municipal Stadium. The team went through a few mentors and list changes, which made it trying to lay out a triumphant custom. Be that as it may, their reliable fan base kept on supporting them through various challenges.

The defining moment for them came in 1943 when they blended momentarily with the Pittsburgh Steelers because of player deficiencies brought about by World War ll. This exceptional course of action, known as the "Steagles," helped support the group's seriousness and established the groundwork for future achievement.

In the last part of the 1940s and mid-1950s, under the authority of lead trainer Earle "Greasy" Neale, the Eagles arrived at new levels. They came out on top for consecutive NFL Titles in 1948 and 1949. These titles denoted the first and, as of my insight cutoff date in September 2021, just NFL titles in the team's set of experiences.

The Eagles' initial years were described by notable players like Steve Van Buren, Chuck Bednarik, and Tommy McDonald, who made a permanent imprint on the establishment and acquired their places in the Pro Football Hall of Fame. The 1960 NFL Title, driven by quarterback Norm Van Brocklin and lead trainer Buck Shaw, was a huge accomplishment and remains a wellspring of pride for Hawks fans.

All through their initial history, the Eagles became known for their energetic and steadfast fan base, who were famous for their commitment to the group. The establishment's unmistakable green and silver tones, alongside the renowned Eagles head logo, became images of Philadelphia sports pride.

Rise to Prominence: 1940s-1970s

The Philadelphia Eagles' rise to fame from the 1940s to the 1970s was a groundbreaking period in the establishment's set of experiences. During these many years, the team took critical steps, making progress and getting through difficulties that would shape its character in the NFL.

During the 1940s, the Eagles saw a striking change under the initiative of lead trainer Earle "Greasy" Neale and the skilled players on the program. The ten years started with a guarantee as the group secured its most memorable NFL Title in 1948. The well-known "Philly Blizzard" title game against the Chicago Cardinals stays at an unbelievable crossroads in Eagles history. This triumph laid out the Eagles as an amazing powerhouse in the NFL.

The 1950s denoted a continuation of the Birds' prosperity, as they got consecutive NFL Titles in 1948 and 1949. The team highlighted remarkable players like Steve Van Buren, Chuck Bednarik, and Tommy McDonald, who assumed essential parts in forming the Eagles' heritage. Bednarik, specifically, turned into a famous figure known for his strength and flexibility, playing both as a linebacker and focus.

In any case, the next many years introduced difficulties for the Eagles, with a time of relative decrease during the 1960s. Despite the promising and less promising times, the team's fan base stayed enthusiastic and strong. This commitment was compensated in 1960 when the Eagles, driven by quarterback Norm Van Brocklin and the "Concrete Charlie" Bednarik, protected their third NFL Title with a noteworthy triumph against the Green Sound Packers.

The 1970s were set apart by changes and advances in the Eagles. An adjustment of possession and the appearance of lead trainer Dick Vermeil reinvigorated the organization. Under Vermeil's initiative, the Falcons started a resurgence that established the groundwork for future achievement. The drafting of headliners like Harold Carmichael and Ron Jaworski restored the team and made them serious in the association.

Modern Era: 1980s to Present

The Philadelphia Eagles have had a captivating journey in the NFL during the cutting-edge period, crossing from the 1980s to the present. This period has been set apart by critical ups and downs, pivotal occasions, and an energetic fan base.

In the mid-1980s, the Eagles encountered a resurgence under lead trainer Dick Vermeil. They arrived at the Super Bowl in the 1980 season yet missed the mark against the Oakland Bandits. This time was remarkable for the "Gang Green" safeguard, which was one of the most considerable in the organization.

The 1990s saw a blend of triumphs and dissatisfactions. The Eagles had serious areas of strength for a consistent yet battled to get a Super Bowl triumph. Eminent players like Reggie White and Randall Cunningham left an enduring effect during this period.

The turn of a thousand years carried another time with lead trainer Andy Reid and quarterback Donovan McNabb. They had an exceptional run of progress, coming to different NFC Title games and lastly arriving at the Super Bowl in the 2004 season. Tragically, they missed the mark against the New England Patriots.

The mid-2000s denoted a progress period, with the team reconstructing and changing the key workforce. The Eagles made a few season-finisher appearances yet couldn't secure another Super Bowl triumph.

During the 2010s, another section started with the appearance of lead trainer Doug Pederson and quarterback Carson Wentz. The Eagles, regardless of confronting accidents with wounds, figured out how to get their most memorable Super Bowl triumph in the 2017 season by overcoming the Nationalists in a significant game.

Backup quarterback Nick Foles assumed a pivotal part and turned into a legend in Philadelphia.

The current time includes continuous endeavors to keep up with intensity and work for what's to come. The team faces difficulties like reconstructing the program and overseeing assumptions from an energetic fan base. The Eagles have shown flexibility and assurance, continuously endeavoring to get back to Super Bowl brilliance.

All through the cutting-edge time, the Philadelphia Eagles have been a basic piece of the NFL's story. Their energetic fan base, notorious players, and paramount minutes have set their position in the organization's set of experiences, and they keep on being a team with a rich heritage and a promising future.

Chapter 2: Key Players and Legends

The Philadelphia Eagles, a team with a rich and celebrated history in the NFL, have seen their reasonable portion of key players and legends throughout the long term.

Hall of Fame Players

Quite possibly one of the most notable figures in the establishment's set of experiences is Chuck Bednarik, who played for the Eagles from 1949 to 1962. Bednarik was a two-way player, succeeding as both a middle on offense and a linebacker on protection. He was known for his strength and was frequently alluded to as "Concrete Charlie." Bednarik's heritage is established by his 10 Master Bowl determinations and two NFL titles with the Eagles in 1949 and 1960.

Another unbelievable Eagle is Reggie White, one of the most predominant protective players in NFL history. White played for the Eagles from 1985 to 1992 and was known as the "Minister of Defense." He was a fearsome pass rusher, recording 124 sacks during his experience with the Falcons and procuring eight Pro Bowl determinations. White's effect reached out past his on-field execution, as he was a vocal leader and powerful figure in the locker room.

Brian Dawkins, a wellbeing who played for the Eagles from 1996 to 2008, is one more famous Hall of Famer. Known for his brutal hits and authority, Dawkins was a nine-time Pro Bowler and was frequently alluded to as

"Weapon X." He was the essence of the Eagles' guard during his residency and stays a cherished figure in Philadelphia sports history.

Moreover, the Eagles have had champion hostile players drafted into the Hall of Fame, including running back Steve Van Buren, who played for the team from 1944 to 1951. Van Buren was a double cross NFL champion and drove the organization in hurrying multiple times. He was a six-time All-Expert choice and was a significant piece of the Eagles' initial success in the NFL.

These are only a couple of the Hall of Fame players who have made a permanent imprint on the Philadelphia Eagles establishment, adding to its celebrated history and energetic fan base.

Memorable Quarterbacks

Perhaps one of the most famous quarterbacks in Eagles history is Donovan McNabb. McNabb was the team's first-round draft pick in 1999, and he proceeded to have an exceptional career with the Eagles. He was known for major areas of strength for him, portability, and capacity to make plays when it made the biggest difference. Under McNabb's authority, the Eagles reliably battled in the NFC, making various journeys to the end of the season games and in any event, arriving at the Super Bowl in the 2004 season. McNabb's career in Philadelphia is set apart by various establishment records and his six Pro Bowl choices.

Another unbelievable Eagles quarterback is Ron Jaworski. " Jaws," as he's lovingly known, was a critical figure for the Eagles during the last part of the 1970s and mid-1980s. He was prestigious for his strength and initiative on the field. Jaworski drove the Eagles to their very first Pro Bowl appearance in the 1980 season, which stands as perhaps the most valued crossroads in the establishment's set of experiences.

Randall Cunningham is another quarterback who holds an extraordinary spot in the Eagles' legend. He was a double-danger quarterback known for his energizing ability to run areas of strength for and. Cunningham's feature reel plays and capacity to improvise made him a fan number one. While he might not have driven the Eagles to a Super Bowl triumph, his effect on the establishment and the association is obvious.

In later years, the Eagles appreciated the accomplishments of Nick Foles, especially during the 2017 season. Foles stepped in for the injured Carson Wentz and drove the team to a staggering Pro Bowl win, procuring Super Bowl MVP praises simultaneously. His "Philly Special" stunt play will always be etched in the Eagles' set of experiences.

The tradition of quarterbacks in Philadelphia Eagles history is rich and diverse, with every one of these signs contributing in extraordinary ways to the team's prosperity. These quarterbacks lastingly impacted the establishment but further charmed themselves to the enthusiastic Eagles fanbase.

Iconic Defensive Players

Quite possibly one of the most notable iconic players in Philadelphia Eagles history is Reggie White. Known as the "Minister of Defense," White was a prevailing power on the Eagles' guarded line from 1985 to 1992. His blend of size, strength, and agility made him a dread for restricting quarterbacks. White was a 13-time Master Bowler, a double cross NFL Defensive Player of the Year, and was enlisted into the Pro Football Hall of Fame in 2006.

Another unbelievable Eagles player is Chuck Bednarik. He was a flexible and hard-core linebacker who played for the Eagles from 1949 to 1962. Bednarik is frequently celebrated for his notable tackle in the 1960 NFL Title Game, where he halted the Giants' Frank Gifford to get the

Eagles' triumph. He was a 10-time Genius Bowler and a critical figure in the Eagles' set of experiences.

Brian Dawkins is one more name that hangs out in the Eagles' defensive Legend. A hard-hitting safety, Dawkins played for Philadelphia from 1996 to 2008. Known for his power and initiative, he procured nine Star Bowl determinations and was a four-time team All-Pro. He is frequently associated with his renowned "Weapon X" persona and his capacity to steer a game with his successes and interferences.

In later years, Fletcher Cox has been a foundation of the Eagle's defense. Cox, a protective tackle, has been a power since being drafted by the Eagles in 2012. He's been named to different Master Bowls and is known for his capacity to disturb contradicting offenses with his pass-hurrying abilities and run-halting ability.

Chapter 3: Memorable Seasons and Championships

In the celebrated history of the Philadelphia Eagles, there have been various essential seasons and titles that have made a permanent imprint on the team and its enthusiastic fanbase.

Super Bowl Triumphs

The Philadelphia Eagles' Super Bowl win in Super Bowl LII, held on February 4, 2018, was a notable crossroads in the establishment's set of experiences. They went head to head against the New England Patriots in a game that charmed football fans the country over.

The Eagles' triumph was a summit of long periods of difficult work and assurance.

They had confronted their portion of highs and lows in the seasons paving the way to Super Bowl LII. With Nick Foles as their quarterback, they entered the postseason as longshots, however still up in the air to discredit the skeptics.

The actual game was a completely exhilarating display, described by hostile firecrackers from the two teams. Nick Foles, specifically, conveyed a wonderful execution, tossing for 373 yards and three scores. The "Philly Special" stunt play, in which Foles got a scoring pass, will be for all time scratched in Super Bowl history.

The Eagles' protection likewise assumed a significant part in their triumph. They figured out how to disturb Tom Brady and the Patriots offense, even though Brady passed for a Super Bowl-record 505 yards.

The game boiled down to the last second, and it was Brandon Graham's strip-sack of Brady late in the final quarter that fixed the Eagles' 41-33 triumph.

Philadelphia fans commended their hotly anticipated Super Bowl win with energy and enthusiasm. The city was decorated with green and white, and the triumph march that followed was an incredible sight. It was a snapshot of unrestrained delight and solidarity for the Eagles' devotion.

Super Bowl LII was not only a football match-up; it was an image of diligence and cooperation. The Eagles' victory will be for the rest of time carved in the chronicles of sports history, filling in as a motivation to fans and hopeful competitors the same. It was a moment of magnificence for the city of Philadelphia and a demonstration of the conviction that with difficult work and assurance, the unimaginable can be accomplished.

NFC Championships

The NFC Title is a significant game in the NFL that decides the meeting champion from the National Football Conference (NFC). This game has had an impact on the NFL end-of-season games, and the victor of the NFC Title acquired the option to address the NFC in the Super Bowl, which is a definitive title game in American football.

The Philadelphia Eagles, situated in Philadelphia, Pennsylvania, have a celebrated history in the NFL and have shown up in the NFC Title throughout the long term. The team is an individual from the NFC East division, which incorporates wild opponents like the Dallas Cowboys, New York Giants, and Washington Football Team.

The Eagles' journey to the NFC Title frequently begins in the normal season, where they go up against individual NFC groups. The result in the ordinary season is basic, as it decides a team's season finisher cultivating. The higher the seed, the more ideal matchups a group can have in the end-of-the-season games.

Once at the end of the season games, the Eagles should explore through different rounds, including the Wild card, Divisional, and eventually, the NFC Title game. The team's presentation in these rounds relies upon a few elements, including the expertise of the players, the training staff's systems, and even factors like weather patterns.

Eagles fans have seen a few critical minutes in the NFC Title throughout the long term. The team has had its portion of wins and heartbreaks, with a few outings to the Super Bowl and Super Bowl triumphs to its name. These triumphs in the NFC Title have frequently been accomplished through the outstanding play of central participants and the devotion of both the training staff and the enthusiastic fan base.

In the NFC Title game, the Eagles face an imposing rival, which could be a serious area of strength for another team with its rich history and goals of arriving at the Super Bowl. The champ of this game not only gets a sought-after spot in the Super Bowl yet, in addition, procures an opportunity to seek the Vince Lombardi

Trophy, quite possibly the most renowned honor in professional football.

The meaning of the NFC Title for the Philadelphia Eagles and their fans couldn't possibly be more significant. It addresses a finish of the time's persistent effort and assurance and offers the potential for brilliance and the satisfaction of dreams. The game is a scene, drawing a huge number of watchers, and the result can be an extremely important occasion in the establishment's set of experiences.

Divisional Dominance

One of the most prominent periods of divisional dominance for the Eagles was during the mid-2000s. Under the authority of lead trainer Andy Reid and with quarterback Donovan McNabb in charge, the Eagles reliably ruled in the NFC East. They secured various division titles and made deep season-finisher runs during this period, including four consecutive NFC Title Game appearances from 2001 to 2004. This degree of supported achievement was a demonstration of the Eagles' strength inside their division.

The Eagles' divisional dominance was portrayed by their standard season accomplishment as well as by their capacity to have a massive impact in the end-of-the-season games. In the 2004 season, they arrived at Super Bowl XIX, at last tumbling to the New England Patriots. Their presence on the NFL's most excellent stage exhibited the strength of the NFC East during that time.

One of the characterizing parts of the Eagles' divisional predominance was their furious contention with the Dallas Cowboys. The fights between these two celebrated establishments enraptured football fans and added to the force of the NFC East. The Eagles' success in the division was in many cases estimated by their capacity to outflank the Cowboys, a contention that keeps on being a point of convergence in the NFL.

The outcome of the Philadelphia Eagles in their division was likewise based on the groundwork of a solid and energetic fan base. Eagles fans, known as the "Philly Faithful," are the absolute most committed and vocal allies in the association. Their immovable obligation to the team created an electric climate at Lincoln Financial Field and added to the team's capacity to keep up with divisional strength.

While the Eagles' divisional strength experienced changes throughout the long term, the team's capacity to transcend their NFC East adversaries at different places in their set of experiences has cemented their place as one of the NFL's most notable establishments. Whether it's their verifiable conflicts with the Cowboys or their vital season-finisher runs, the Philadelphia Eagles' divisional strength stays a critical section in the chronicles of NFL history.

Chapter 4: The Eagles' Fanbase and Culture

The Philadelphia Eagles, a celebrated establishment in the NFL, are characterized by their on-field accomplishment as well as by the energetic and special fanbase that upholds them.

Dedicated Fan Groups

Dedicated fan groups assume a fundamental part in the realm of pro athletics, creating a feeling of local area, energy, and solidarity among fans. The Philadelphia Eagles brag about one of the most intense and devoted fan bases in all of sports. This fan base is known for its faithfulness, particular practices, and the immovable help of its adored group.

One of the most notable parts of Philadelphia Eagles fan culture is the enthusiastic and rambunctious climate at Lincoln Financial Field, their home arena. Eagles fans are well known for their vivacious closely-following gatherings, where they accumulate hours before the opening shot to cook, share stories, and take part in amicable talk. The kinship among fans is substantial, making an extraordinary and electric game-day experience.

The Eagles' committed fan bases come in many structures, from neighborhood promoter clubs to worldwide web-based networks. These gatherings frequently arrange occasions, get-togethers, and beneficent drives that mirror their profound obligation to the group. The "Philly Faithful" and "Eagles Nest Outlaws" are two noticeable instances of fan bunches that effectively support the Hawks. These associations frequently organize journeys to away games, transforming contradicting arenas into an ocean of green as they show their loyalty regardless of location.

The commitment of Eagles fans reaches out past game days. They enthusiastically follow each part of the group, from draft day to the offseason. The yearly NFL Draft is an occasion enthusiastically expected by fans, as they accumulate in huge numbers to watch the determinations and examine their possible effect on the group. Likewise, the free office time frame and preseason games are met with energy and hypothesis by the fan base.

Maybe the most famous custom in the Eagles' fan culture is the "Eagles Fight

Song." Sung uproariously and gladly before and after each game, this custom joins fans and reverberates all through the city. The verses, "Fly, Eagles, Fly," have become inseparable from the team's soul and determination.

Web-based entertainment and online gatherings have additionally intensified the feeling of local area among Eagles fans. These stages empower fans to share their considerations, feelings, and backing for the team. It's normal to see Eagles fans participating in vivacious discussions about the group's presentation, examining their number one players, or thinking back about notable crossroads in establishment history.

Eagles fan bases likewise participate in charitable exercises, mirroring the local area soul that penetrates the fan base. From good cause drives to charitable efforts, these gatherings utilize their enthusiasm for the Eagles to have a beneficial outcome in the more prominent Philadelphia region. The Eagles Autism Challenge, for example, is a magnanimous occasion firmly connected with the team, raising assets for mental imbalance research, and many fan bases effectively take part and back this reason.

Tailgating Traditions

One of the champion parts of Eagles closely following is the food culture. Fans invest wholeheartedly in their culinary manifestations, exhibiting a wide cluster of heavenly dishes. From exemplary Philly cheesesteaks to creative following recipes, the smell of barbecuing meats and appetizing treats consumes the space. It's normal to see fans trading recipes and barbecuing tips, making a feeling of the local area through the craft of cooking.

Philadelphia Eagles backends are also known for their lively pre-game ceremonies. Fans accumulate hours before the opening shot, setting up intricate tents and barbecuing stations. The climate is energetic, with music booming, fans messing around like cornhole and brew pong, and children throwing footballs around, retaining the infectious energy.

The brotherhood among Eagles fans is substantial. Outsiders become quick companions, holding over shared triumphs and losses. The rear-end parties act as a blend of different people, joined by their adoration for the Eagles. Fans clad in green and white offer stories, giggling, and once in a while even well-disposed chit chat with restricting group allies, making a one-of-a-kind mix of contention and regard

Cooperation is one more fundamental component of the Eagles' rear ends. Fans gladly show their team dependability through intricate ensembles, face painting, and specially crafted pennants. The sea of green and white is something else, displaying the resolute commitment of Eagles allies. Serenades and cheers resonate through the parking areas, repeating the energy of the fans and building a staggering air of solidarity.

The Eagles' back end likewise has a charitable side. Many fan bases coordinate magnanimous occasions and pledge drives during game days, utilizing the get-togethers of enthusiastic fans to have a beneficial outcome in the local area. These drives feature the empathetic side of Eagles's allies, exhibiting their obligation to offer in return and having an effect past the football field.

Impact on Philadelphia's Community

Past the bounds of the football field, the Eagles have woven themselves into the social texture of the city, making a permanent imprint on its inhabitants.

One of the main impacts of the Eagles on the Philadelphia people group is the feeling of solidarity and pride they motivate. At the point when the Eagles play, the whole city meets up, paying little mind to race, religion, or financial foundation. The games act as a revitalizing point, encouraging a feeling of having a place among different gatherings. This solidarity is maybe best exemplified during the Eagles' noteworthy Super Bowl triumph in 2018. The festivals that followed rose above ordinary ballyhoo; they turned into a public articulation of delight, bringing people from varying backgrounds together in a common snapshot of win.

Besides, the Eagles' drives have had a significant effect on the existence of numerous Philadelphians. The team has reliably been engaged with different local area outreach programs, resolving issues like instruction, neediness, and medical services. Through these drives, the Eagles have decidedly influenced the existence of oppressed youth, giving them potential open doors and assets they could not, in any case, have approached.

The team's impact additionally reaches out to the neighborhood economy. Home games attract a large number of fans to Lincoln Financial Field, producing income for neighboring organizations and making positions inside the local area. Also, the Eagles' prosperity on the field has helped the city's travel industry, drawing in guests who need to encounter the energy of an Eagle game and explore the city that upholds them. Besides, the Eagles act as good examples for trying competitors, ingraining areas of strength for an ethic and a feeling of devotion. Youthful fans admire players as legends, for their ability on the field, yet in addition for their commitments off the field. This impact empowers the young people of Philadelphia to think beyond practical boundaries and endeavor to accomplish their objectives, encouraging a culture of desire and assurance.

Chapter 5: Iconic Rivalries

In the realm of American expert football, scarcely any rivalries are around as celebrated and extreme as the Philadelphia Eagles' competitions. These fights on the field have caught the hearts and psyches of fans for ages, characterizing the actual embodiment of contest and energy in the game.

Historic Battles with Dallas Cowboys

These two teams have quite possibly the most extraordinary competition in the organization, with matchups that have been anxiously expected by fans for a long time. Perhaps the most essential rivalry between the Eagles and Cowboys occurred in 1980. The Eagles, driven by lead trainer Dick

Vermeil and star quarterback Ron Jaworski, faced the Cowboys in the NFC Title Game. The Eagles came out triumphant, getting their most memorable Super Bowl appearance. This success is scratched in the recollections of Eagles fans as a victorious crossroads in the competition's set of experiences.

During the 1990s, the Cowboys, under the direction of lead trainer Jimmy Johnson and driven by the "Triplets" - Troy Aikman, Emmitt Smith, and Michael Irvin - dominated the NFL. The Eagles, then again, confronted various difficulties. Be that as it may, this period saw serious fights between the two teams, with the two sides exchanging blows and competing for incomparability in the NFC East.

The 2000s brought a resurgence for the Eagles under lead trainer Andy Reid. Donovan McNabb, an establishment quarterback, drove the team to a few season finisher appearances and a Super Bowl billet in the 2004 season. The competition with the Cowboys strayed wild, as the two teams kept on areas of strength for handling, making their matchups a point of convergence of the NFL season.

Outstanding games between the Eagles and Cowboys frequently included emotional rebounds, last-minute heroics, and questionable minutes. These games have made a permanent imprint on the convention's set of experiences. The energetic fan bases of the two teams, with Eagles fans known for their devotion and Cowboys fans for their "America's Team" status, simply added to the power of these fights.

As we move into the current day, the notable rivalry between the Eagles and Dallas Cowboys keeps on dazzling football fans. Each season, the matchups between these two teams are orbited on the schedule as must-watch games, and the result stays eccentric, keeping the soul of the contest alive.

Intense Matchups with the New York Giants

These games are challenges of expertise and procedure as well as clashes of pride and custom.

One of the main parts of this competition is the nearness of the two urban areas, both situated in the thickly populated northeastern US. This geological closeness adds a layer of power to their experiences, as fans from the two teams frequently blend and conflict, making a discernible strain in the arenas.

By and large, the Giants and the Eagles have frequently been comparable to one another as far as generally speaking achievement, making their matchups even more significant. The fights have delivered vital minutes that are carved into the chronicles of NFL history.

Incredible players like Lawrence Taylor, Michael Strahan, and Eli Manning have influenced these experiences for the Giants, while the Eagles have seen stars like Reggie White, Chuck Bednarik, and Brian Dawkins lead their charge. These people have embodied the savage contest and enthusiastic nature of this competition.

Strikingly, games between these two teams have frequently had season-finisher suggestions, adding significantly greater force to their conflicts. With division titles and postseason compartments much of the time in limbo, the results of these matchups altogether affect the more extensive NFL scene.

The MetLife Stadium in East Rutherford, New Jersey, and Lincoln Financial Field in Philadelphia have facilitated a considerable lot of these extraordinary experiences, creating a phase where the enthusiasm and competition between the teams and their fans are on full display.

As of late, the competition has seen its portion of exciting, possible minute fights, where games have been chosen in the end minutes, further powering the hostility and enthusiasm between the teams and their allies.

Fierce Feuds with Washington Football Team

This rivalry is described by serious rivalry, paramount minutes, and enthusiastic fan bases on the two sides.

Quite possibly the most notable second in this fight happened in 1990 when the Eagles crushed Washington, taking them out of season finisher conflict and getting a season finisher spot for themselves. This game, known as the "Body Gag Game," highlighted the Eagles' safeguard persistently terminating Washington's quarterbacks, prompting a stunning nine quarterback sacks in a solitary game. It turned into a vital crossroads in the competition's legend.

Over time, the two teams have had their portion of progress, and their no-holds-barred matchups have frequently had huge season-finisher suggestions. The groups have met two times every year as a component of the NFC East division, heightening their contention as they battle for divisional incomparability.

The competition reaches out past the football field and into the stands. Eagles fans, infamous for their enthusiasm and in some cases wild way of behaving, have a long history of provoking Washington fans and players. Similarly, Washington fans have not been timid about communicating their contempt for the Eagles.

Off the field, the competition has seen its reasonable part of discussions. The name and mascot of the Washington Football Team were the subjects of contention and conversations about social responsiveness, prompting an adjustment of the group's name and marking. This change added one more layer of intricacy to the contention, as the Eagles needed to adjust to another name and character for their divisional enemy.

Despite the changes, the rivalry keeps on being a feature of the NFL season, with the two teams and their fans enthusiastically expecting the standoffs. These games are set apart by hard hits, sensational rebounds, and the unusual idea of divisional matchups.

Chapter 6: Behind the Scenes: Team Management

Fruitful NFL teams, similar to the Eagles, depend vigorously on the productive coordination and the executives of their players, mentors, and support staff.

Coaching Dynasties

The Philadelphia Eagles, while not generally connected with the expression "dynasty," have had their reasonable portion of outstanding instructing times that left an enduring effect on the establishment.

One of the most unmistakable training traditions in the Eagles' set of experiences can be followed back to the mid-2000s. Under the direction of lead trainer Andy Reid, the team encountered a time of reliable seriousness. Reid, known for his hostile ability, stood firm on the footing for 14 seasons, from 1999 to 2012. During his residency, the Eagles made various season-finisher appearances, remembering a Super Bowl appearance for the 2004 season. Even though they missed the mark in that title game, the Reid time was set apart by strength and greatness, with players like Donovan McNabb and Brian Westbrook becoming notable figures in Philadelphia sports history.

One more remarkable section in the Eagles' training history unfurled when Chip Kelly assumed control in 2013. Kelly carried an inventive hostile way of dealing with the NFL, integrating components of his fruitful school-instructing career. His quick-moving, team offense made a buzz in the organization, and for a short period, it seemed like the Eagles were on the cusp of another time. While Kelly's residency was somewhat fleeting, it made an imprint on the establishment's hostile way of thinking.

The most recent training line that collected critical consideration was under Doug Pederson, who took over in 2016. Pederson's initiative finished in a Super Bowl triumph in the 2017 season, denoting the first title in Eagles set of experiences. His striking dynamic in the Super Bowl, including the "Philly Special" stunt play, became an unbelievable Philadelphia sports legend. Pederson's capacity to revitalize the group and conform to misfortune was a sign of his training style.

Every one of these training lines, while particular in their methods, added to the

Eagles' heritage in their specific manner. They addressed various times and ways of thinking in the consistently developing scene of the NFL. The pitch of training lines lies in the gathering of prizes as well as in their effect on the way of life, character, and custom of an establishment, and the Eagles have seen a few striking sections in their set of experiences that have formed their personality in proficient football.

Front Office Strategies

One of the key procedures utilized by the Eagles' front office is information-driven navigation. Through cutting-edge inspection and player execution measurements, the team's administration recognizes likely ability, assesses player adequacy, and goes with vital choices on player agreements, exchanges, and draft determinations.

Despite information inspection, the Eagles center around compensation cap the board. Exploring the complex NFL compensation cap framework is urgent for supporting a cutthroat program. The front office, driven by experienced leaders, decisively dispenses assets to hold center players while additionally investigating financially savvy choices in a free organization and the draft to fill holes and reinforce the group.

The ability to explore and improve assumes a critical part of the Eagle's front-office method. The team puts resources into exploring organizations and ability evaluators to recognize promising players in school football and other expert associations. Whenever players are brought into the Eagles association, there are serious areas of strength for on-player improvement. This includes giving players repairing offices and assets to upgrade their abilities and amplify their true capacity.

Moreover, the Eagle's focus is on coordinated effort and collaboration inside their front office. Powerful equality and collaboration among mentors, scouts, examiners, and directors are fundamental for adjusting the team's vision and objectives. Standard gatherings and meetings to generate new ideas cultivate a climate where creative thoughts are shared, prompting informed choices that benefit the group in both the short and long haul.

Versatility is one more sign of the Birds' front office procedures. The NFL scene is continually advancing, with rule changes, recent fads, and changes in player inclinations. The Eagles' administration stays adaptable and adjusts its techniques to take advantage of rising open doors. Whether it's changing the course of action mid-season or taking vital actions in the offseason, the front office is constantly ready to turn because of evolving conditions.

Plus, the Eagles focus on local area commitment and fan relations. Building areas of strength for the fan base improves the team's image as well as creates a steady climate that can lift player confidence level and execution. Through different local area drives, outreach projects, and fan occasions, the Eagles' front office encourages a feeling of having a place and pride among allies, making a good criticism circle that benefits both the team and its steadfast fanbase.

Player Development and Drafting

The Eagles have areas of strength for putting resources into player improvement. They comprehend that the way to support achievement isn't simply getting capable players through the draft but also sustaining and refining their abilities once they're on the team. This obligation to player improvement has been obvious in their predictable endeavors to establish a helpful climate for development.

One of the characterizing highlights of the Eagles' player improvement system is their dependence on a powerful instructing staff. They have generally recruited experienced and imaginative mentors who can draw out the best in their players. Fostering players' essentials and leveling up their abilities is a main concern. The team's formative projects, both in-season and during the off-season, are intended to address the particular necessities of every player, assisting them with arriving at their maximum capacity.

The Eagles have likewise been proactive in cultivating a culture of contest inside the group. They comprehend that opposition among players pushes everybody to get to the next level. The act of vacant position fights guarantees that players are constantly tested to demonstrate their value, and this, thus, prods development.

As far as drafting, the Eagles have utilized a scope of methodologies throughout the long term. Their way of thinking has for the most part been to track down the most ideal that anyone could hope to find ability while additionally considering their particular team needs. The draft can be erratic, and the Eagles have adjusted to different circumstances by being adaptable and light-footed in their method.

One vital accomplishment for the Eagles has been their capacity to uncover unlikely treasures in the draft. They have a history of recognizing late-round or undrafted players who later become key supporters of the team. This skill for finding gems waiting to be discovered addresses their exploring division's aptitude.

Furthermore, the Eagles have taken striking actions in the draft when vital. Their choice to exchange up for Carson Wentz in 2016 is a perfect representation. While the consequences of such moves can be blended, they show an eagerness to make huge wagers in the quest for an establishment quarterback or a game-evolving ability.

Challenges have additionally emerged in the Eagles' player advancement and drafting history. The change to another training staff or front office can disturb the congruity of player improvement. Changes in administration can bring about various assessment measures, prompting potential befuddles between player acquisitions and improvement programs.

The team has in some cases confronted analysis for its draft choices. Like some other NFL establishment, the Eagles have encountered their portion of draft busts, which can interfere with the team's advancement. Adjusting the requirement for sure-fire influence with long-haul potential is a continuous test in the draft.

Chapter 7: Impact on the NFL and Pop Culture

The Philadelphia Eagles have made a permanent imprint on the NFL and mainstream society, both on and off the field.

Eagles in Popular Media

Past their on-field accomplishments, the group's logo, colors, and wild standing have tracked down their direction into different types of amusement, from films to Programs and even music.

In motion pictures, the Eagles have been highlighted in a few movies that catch the substance of football culture. One outstanding model is the 2006 games show film "Invincible," featuring Imprint

Wahlberg. The film recounts the motivating genuine story of Vince Papale, a barkeep who turned into an individual from the Eagles during the 1970s. "Invincible" not only grandstands the coarseness and assurance of the team but also illustrates Philadelphia's well-established association with its football crew.

Besides, the Eagles have been referred to in various Television programs, turning into an image of the city's pride. In the famous sitcom "It's Always Sunny in Philadelphia," the principal characters frequently go to Eagles games, exhibiting the team's impact on the city's social texture. The show catches the enthusiasm and in some cases unreasonable way of behaving of dedicated Eagles fans, featuring the group's social importance in Philadelphia.

Past the domain of visual media, the Eagles have additionally transformed music. The band Eagles, named after the notable flying predator, accomplished overall popularity with their exemplary hits. While the band's name doesn't straightforwardly reference the football crew, the imagery of the bird as a strong and superb animal reverberates with the group's picture, further establishing the Eagles' social importance.

Despite fictitious portrayals, the Eagles' players and their accounts have been highlighted in narratives and true-to-life films. These creations give a brief look into the existences of the players, displaying their battles, wins, and the steady soul that characterizes the Falcons collectively.

Influence on NFL Policies

One huge area of impact has been their way of dealing with local area commitment. The Eagles have been at the front of social drives, utilizing their foundation to resolve different cultural issues. Through programs zeroed in on training, well-being, and civil rights, the group has set a norm for different establishments, provoking the NFL to take on association-wide drives that advance local area contribution.

Besides, the Eagles' prosperity on the field has likewise formed NFL arrangements. Their procedures in ability procurement and grouping the board have been firmly seen by different establishments. The "Philly Special," a stunt play that became notable after the Birds involved it in Super Bowl LII, propelled a rush of imagination among mentors across the association. This creative soul has urged the NFL to embrace capricious strategies, encouraging a seriously intriguing and erratic game for fans.

As far as player government assistance, the Eagles have been advocates for upgraded security measures. Their obligation to player well-being and prosperity, proved by interests in state-of-the-art preparing offices and clinical staff, has impacted the association's conventions concerning injury anticipation and recuperation. The NFL, in light of such drives, has persistently refreshed its blackout conventions and put resources into exploration to guarantee player security stays a main concern.

Furthermore, the Eagles' fanbase, known for its energetic help, has prompted conversations about fan commitment techniques inside the NFL. The team's endeavors to interface with fans through web-based entertainment, local area occasions, and intuitive encounters have prodded an association-wide spotlight on upgrading the general fan insight. From computerized developments to arena conveniences, the NFL has embraced a fan-first methodology, recognizing the significance of a committed and drawn-in crowd.

Also, the Eagles' outcome in advancing variety and consideration inside their association has provoked the NFL to resolve issues of portrayal. By encouraging a different front office and training staff, the Eagles have become pioneers in advancing open doors for underrepresented gatherings.

This obligation to variety has impacted the NFL's employing strategies, empowering a more comprehensive methodology across all groups.

Eagles' Players in the Hall of Fame

The Philadelphia Eagles, a celebrated establishment in the NFL, have seen a few of their unbelievable players cherished in the Hall of Fame. These people have made critical commitments to the group's set of experiences and have made a permanent imprint on the game. We should dig into a portion of the Eagles' Iconic Hall of Famers:

Chuck Bednarik: Frequently viewed as one of the hardest and most diligent players in NFL history, Hurl Bednarik played for the Eagles from 1949 to 1962. He was a two-way player, succeeding as a middle on offense and a linebacker on guard. Bednarik's unbelievable hit on Candid Gifford of the New York Giants in 1960 remains one of the most famous crossroads in NFL history.

Reggie White: Known as the "Minister of Defense," Reggie White was a prevailing power on the Eagles' cautious line during his residency from 1985 to 1992. He was a double cross NFL Cautious Player of the Year and recorded a momentous 124 sacks as a Bird.

Steve Van Buren: Considered one of the early stars of the NFL, Steve Van Buren was a flexible running back who played for the Eagles from 1944 to 1951. He was a three-time NFL hurrying boss and assumed a significant part in the Eagles' consecutive NFL Titles in 1948 and 1949.

Tommy McDonald: Tommy McDonald was a powerful wide receiver who enjoyed seven seasons with the Eagles from 1957 to 1963. His speed, deftness, and capacity to make gymnastics made him a fan #1. McDonald was a six-time Pro Bowler and assumed a huge part in the Eagles' 1960 NFL Title.

Brian Dawkins: Known for his savage hits and unparalleled enthusiasm for the game, Brian Dawkins was a foundation of the Eagles' safeguard for north of 10 years, from 1996 to 2008. He was a nine-time Expert Bowler and turned into the close-to-home head of the team during their effective years.

These Hall of Famers are only a couple of the eminent players who have worn the Philadelphia Eagles' uniform and added to the establishment's rich history. Their impact on the team, the city, and the NFL all in all is irrefutable, and they keep on being praised as symbols of the game.

Chapter 8: Looking Forward: Challenges and Aspirations

The establishment's rich history and getting through fan base have made way for an intriguing journey ahead.

Recent Developments and Team Changes

The Philadelphia Eagles have encountered a critical change in initiative and player elements lately. Strikingly, in mid-2021, the Eagles headed out in different directions from lead trainer Doug Pederson, who had been a conspicuous figure in the establishment's new achievement, including the Super Bowl win in 2017. This was the start of another time, with Nick Sirianni taking over as the lead trainer, carrying new thoughts and procedures to the group.

Quite possibly one of the most vital changes has been the progress at the quarterback position. Carson Wentz, when seen as the establishment quarterback, experienced a progression of battles, including wounds and execution issues. Thus, he was exchanged to the Indianapolis Colts during the 2021 offseason.

Jalen Hurts, a youthful and promising quarterback, assumed control as the starter, and the organization has been centered around his improvement as a key structure block for what's to come.

The 2021 NFL Draft carried energy to Eagles fans as the team chose DeVonta Smith, a zapping wide beneficiary from Alabama, as the tenth general pick. Smith's expansion has supported the getting corps and furnished Hurts with a significant objective. The choice of Smith flagged the association's obligation to build an intriguing and intense offense around their young sign guest.

On the edge side, the Eagles went through changes too. While veterans like Brandon Graham kept on being fundamental supporters, the team acquainted more youthful gifts with reinforcing the protection, zeroing in on a blend of involvement and potential.

Wounds introduced a critical test to the group's consistency, especially in the out-attack mode line. These wounds impacted the Eagles and required versatility and strength from the training staff and players to explore the difficulties.

Fan Expectations and Team Goals

Philadelphia Eagles fans, eminent for their energy and immovable help, have consistently held elevated standards for their group. These assumptions are well established in the rich history of the establishment, including the notorious Super Bowl LII triumph that carried monstrous pride to the city. With a heritage based on devotion and wins, fans expect nothing not as much as greatness from their darling Eagles.

At the center of fan assumptions lies the craving for predictable achievement. Eagles allies enthusiastically expect to excite matchups, amazing plays, and, in particular, triumphs. The fans long for serious areas of strength for a group that epitomizes the soul of Philadelphia, not set in stone, and unfaltering. They shift focus over to the players as competitors as well as images of their local area, anticipating that they should address the city with satisfaction and respectability on and off the field.

At the same time, the actual team lays out aggressive objectives lined up with the intense goals of its fans. The essential goal is to secure another Super Bowl title. The excitement to remember the elation of the 2018 Super Bowl triumph powers the group's assurance. Yet again every season, players and instructing staff are driven by the quest for greatness, planning to come to the end of the season games as well as to go as far as possible and lift the Lombardi Prize.

Also, the Eagles go for the gold exhibition. They seek to overwhelm their division, laying down a good foundation for themselves as an awe-inspiring phenomenon in the profoundly cutthroat NFC East. Accomplishing this requires fastidious preparation, thorough preparation, and a vital dynamic in both player acquisitions and game strategies. The team's objective isn't simply flashing achievement, however, it supported greatness over numerous seasons.

Moreover, the Eagles focus on the improvement of youthful abilities. Putting resources into the future by sustaining promising players is a key goal. Philadelphia fans figure out the meaning of serious areas of strength for a list and enthusiastically expect the rise of new stars who will carry the group forward.

Off the field, local area commitment stays a key objective for the Eagles association.

They endeavor to have constructive success on the existence of their fans and the more extensive Philadelphia people team through different effort programs and beneficent drives. This obligation to social obligation resounds deeply with the fans, who invest heavily in supporting a group that thinks often about the prosperity of its local area.

Conclusion

Philadelphia Eagles stand as a celebrated and tough establishment in the realm of expert football. With a rich history that traces back to 1933, the group has gone through its reasonable part of high points and low points, confronting difficulties and accomplishing wonderful triumphs. They have made a permanent imprint on the NFL and the hearts of their devoted fan base.

Throughout the long term, the Eagles have reliably shown their obligation to greatness on the field. Prominently, they captured their most memorable Super Bowl title in the 2017-2018 season, denoting a noteworthy crossroads in the establishment's set of experiences. This accomplishment was the height of long periods of difficult work, devotion, and the steady help of their fans.

Past the successes and accidents, they have been prestigious for their enthusiastic and faithful fan base. Philadelphia's fans, frequently alluded to as the "Eagles Nation," are known for their commitment and unflinching help, filling Lincoln Financial Field with energy and pride on game days.

The team has likewise been home to amazing players and mentors who have left a permanent heritage in the game of football. Names like Chuck Bednarik, Reggie White, Brian Dawkins, and Donovan McNabb are perpetually carved in the archives of NFL history, addressing the Eagles with unique excellence.

Despite their on-field achievement, the Eagles have shown a guarantee to their local area, participating in different magnanimous undertakings and beneficent exercises. Their endeavors off the field decidedly affect the city of Philadelphia and then some.

As the Eagles proceed to develop and adjust to the changing scene of expert football, one thing stays steady: their enthusiastic and committed fan base. The Philadelphia Eagles are not only a football crew; they are an image of strength, local area, and relentless help. Their heritage in the NFL will proceed to develop, and their effect on the game and the city of Philadelphia will endure for a long time into the future.

Printed in Great Britain
by Amazon